THE
NATURAL WORLD

STORNOWAY PRIMARY

WESTERN ISLES LIBRARIES

Readers are requested to take great care of the books while in their
possession, and to point out any defects that they may notice in them
to the Librarian.
This book is issued for a period of twenty-one days and should be
returned on or before the latest date stamped below, but an extension
of the period of loan may be granted when desired.

DATE OF RETURN	DATE OF RETURN	DATE OF RETURN

THE
NATURAL WORLD
through the eyes of artists

Windsor Castle, Royal Library © Her Majesty The Queen

Wendy and Jack Richardson

MACMILLAN

First published 1989

Published by Macmillan Children's Books
A division of MACMILLAN PUBLISHERS LTD.
Houndmills, Basingstoke, Hampshire RG21 2XS and London

Companies and representatives throughout the world

Picture research by Faith Perkins

Printed in Italy

British Library Cataloguing in Publication Data

Richardson, Wendy
The Natural World
I. Graphic Arts. Special subjects. Nature.
I. Title II. Richardson, Jack III series
760'. 0443

ISBN 0-333-47569-0

Photographic acknowledgements
The authors and publishers wish to acknowledge with thanks the following photographic sources:

Cover: Hunters in the Snow – Kunsthistorisches Museum, Vienna (The Bridgeman Art Library)

Spray of Oak Leaves and Dyer's Greenweed – Windsor Castle, Royal Library © Her Majesty The Queen p iii
Antelopes – (Visual Publications Ltd) p vi
Brueghel – (The Mansell Collection) p 8
Hunters in the Snow – Kunsthistorisches Museum, Vienna (The Bridgeman Art Library) p 9
Misty Morning – Musée d'Orsay, Paris (The Bridgeman Art Library) p 11
John Everett Millais – The National Portrait Gallery, London p 12
Winter Fuel – City Art Gallery, Manchester p 13
Pissarro – Giraudon, Paris p 14
The Côte des Boeufs – The National Gallery, London p 15
Colin Lanceley – p 16
Songs of a Summer Night © Colin Lanceley p 17
John Constable – The National Portrait Gallery, London p 18
Salisbury Cathedral from the Meadows – The National Gallery, London p 19
John Piper – Photograph March – Penny (Camera Press) p 20
Newcastle Emlyn The Tate Gallery, London p 21
Dali – Photograph Len Sirman (Camera Press) p 22
The Solar Table – Museum Boymans-van Beuningen, Rotterdam © DEMART PRO ARTE BV 1988 p 23
Arthur Boyd – (Photograph Jorge Lewinski) p 24
Santa Gertrudis Bull – Reproduced by kind permission of Patricia Boyd p 25
Cézanne – The Phillips Collection, Washington p 26
Mont Sainte Victoire – The Phillips Collection, Washington p 27
Gauguin – National Gallery of Art, Washington. The Chester Dale Collection p 28
Landscape with Peacocks – Pushkin Museum, Moscow (Novosti) p 29
John Singer Sargent – The Tate Gallery, London p 30
Mountain Fire – The Brooklyn Museum, Brooklyn p 31
Antelopes – (Visual Publications Ltd) p 33
Plate of White Beans – Palatina, Florence (Scala) p 35
Courbet – The National Gallery, London p 36
Still Life: Apples and Pomegranates – The National Gallery, London p 37
Pomegranate Tree – (Aurora Art Publishers, USSR) p 39
René Magritte – © Lee Miller Archives p 40
The Listening Room – Private Collection © ADAGP, Paris/ DACS London 1988 (The Bridgeman Art Library) p 41
Flowers and Shells – Staatliche Kunstsammlungen, Dresden (Photo Gerhard – Reinhold) p 43
Odilon Redon – Musée d'Orsay, Paris (Service Photographique de la Reunion des Musées nationaux) p 44
Flowers in a Green Vase – Carnegie Institute Museum of Art, Pittsburgh, Pennsylvania, (The Bridgeman Art Library) p 45
Monet – The Tate Gallery, London © DACS 1988 p 46
Massif de Chrysanthèmes – Kunstmuseum, Basel. The Emile Dreyfus Foundation © DACS 1988 (Photo Hans Hinz) p 47

The publishers have made every effort to trace the copyright holders, but if they have inadvertently overlooked any, they will be pleased to make the necessary arrangements at the first opportunity.

Introduction

This is a book of pictures about the natural world. Some of the paintings are old and some of them have been painted quite recently. They come from many parts of the world.

All the pictures look very different, but they have one thing in common. They were painted by people who had an idea about nature and thought that the best way to share it was through a picture. So this is a book for you to look at.

The pictures tell how the artists felt about the many wonders of nature. There are pictures of mountains and valleys, of day-time and night-time, of flowers and plants. Some are very careful, accurate drawings and some are very imaginative. Some will delight you, some puzzle you and some may even seem frightening. Take a careful look at the pictures to see if you can find out what the painters hoped to tell us through their work.

Contents

Hunters in the Snow (January)

Oil paint on wood panel 117 × 162 cm

Pieter Brueghel

LIVED:
about 1525-1569

NATIONALITY:
Flemish

TYPE OF WORK:
paintings, engravings

The details of Pieter Brueghel's early life are not known, but he was probably apprenticed to a painter who had studios in Brussels and Antwerp. We do know that he travelled to Italy in 1552 and 1553, visiting Naples and Rome. Brueghel died when he was about forty-four years old, and fifty of his paintings survive today.

This painting is part of a set of twelve paintings, each one showing a month of the year. All but five of the paintings have been lost. This one, showing January, is now a very popular picture, but Brueghel's work has not always been so popular. For a long time he was thought of as a painter of ugly scenes and ugly people, and he was known by the nickname 'Peasant Brueghel'. He did not follow the styles of other painters of his time, who made everything they painted look beautiful.

A speedy worker

Brueghel probably painted all twelve pictures of the months in less than one year. He worked quickly, using thin paint, and he often allowed the undercoat on the wooden panel to show through the oil paint. The undercoat was a brilliant white mixture of chalky pigment and glue, called *gesso*, which was applied in several layers to the wood.

A day to chill you

It might be expected that a picture of a cold day would be painted in cold, blueish colours but Brueghel has not chosen those. Everything here has the yellowish tone of those damp, dull January days when the snow has become dreary and dirty. The snow reflects the heavy cloud which seems to squash down on the Earth and close the world in like a suffocating blanket.

Brueghel cleverly uses a change in the sizes of figures and buildings to give a sense of distance from the hunters in the foreground. The winding river helps as well. In the distance trees and houses are dimly seen. They are little more than shadows on the harsh landscape, yet Brueghel's skilled brush leaves us in no doubt as to the meaning of his marks. The stark silhouettes of the trees and the birds which are so easily visible on the leafless branches give a hard edge to this harsh day.

January is revealed like a story as you read the picture.

Kunsthistorisches Museum, Vienna

Misty Morning

Oil on canvas 50 × 65 cm

Alfred Sisley

LIVED:
1839-1899

NATIONALITY:
British

TYPE OF WORK:
oil paintings

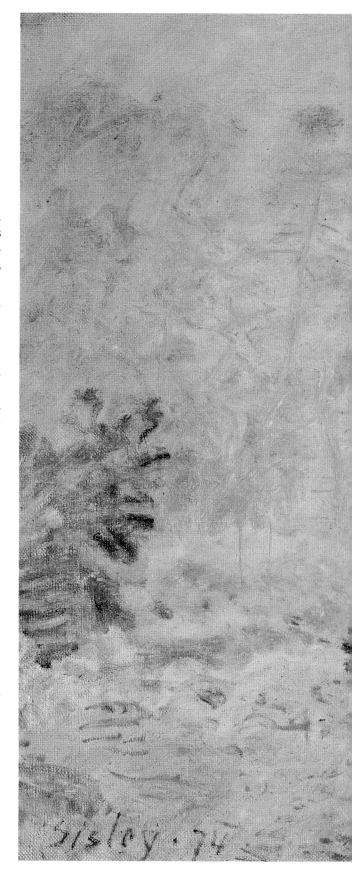

Though Alfred Sisley's parents were British he was born in France. He spent four years in London when he was between eighteen and twenty-two years old, but he regarded France as his homeland. When he returned to Paris he persuaded his parents to let him study painting. For the next ten years Sisley was supported by his father, during which time he was able to paint full time.

The beginning of Impressionism

Sisley studied at the studio of a Swiss painter, Gleyre, and there he met three young men, Monet, Renoir and Bazille. Together they discussed their work and their ideas about a new way of seeing and painting which was to become known as Impressionism.

The pictures were based on close observation of nature and were usually painted out of doors in direct contact with the subject. For many years the Impressionists' work was mocked and ridiculed by art critics. Whilst his father could support him Sisley's life was fairly comfortable, but when the family fortunes were lost, Sisley had to make his living by selling his work. Sadly, it was only in the year in which Sisley died that his pictures began to be appreciated. Within a few years of his death they sold for high prices, but Sisley died in poverty, in the little town in the country which had been his home for nearly twenty years.

A gentle style

This painting was made when Sisley was still living near Paris. It is a quietly coloured, gentle scene, full of atmosphere. We can feel the silence that the mist brings, isolating the woman working in her garden.

Sisley never changed his style. He worked in soft colours using tiny brush strokes. He did not draw in detail exactly what the eye would see from close up, but gave the impression of a scene which we see from a distance. In this picture the mist blurs the shapes, and we peer over the flowerbed and the cabbage patch. What might we see beyond the fence when the mist clears?

Winter Fuel

Oil on canvas 194.3 × 149.8 cm

John Everett Millais

LIVED:
1829-1896

NATIONALITY:
British

TYPE OF WORK:
paintings, book illustrations

The National Portrait Gallery, London

John Everett Millais was, at eleven years old, the youngest student ever to attend the Royal Academy of Art in London. There he met the painters Holman Hunt and Rossetti. They formed a group, sharing their ideas of painting and calling themselves the Pre-Raphaelite Brotherhood. They aimed to paint directly from nature, paying attention to detail and using natural objects in their pictures as symbols for ideas. Their work was not much liked by the public at first, but Millais' work soon became very popular. His rather sentimental pictures appealed to the Victorian public. This painting and four others were sold in 1874 for £10 000, a great deal of money in those days.

Popular but true to himself

Critics have sometimes said that Millais wasted his wonderful talent. They thought that he chose easy, popular subjects that would earn him money, but Millais did not change his way of painting whatever he painted. This painting was one of a set of landscapes of Scotland. Millais worked out of doors, paying great attention to the detail of his subject. Look at the bark of the silver birch tree trunk, for example, to see how Millais builds up the picture using tiny brush strokes.

This is a late autumn picture. The last leaves cling to the cut branches, but the trees on the mountain-side are still richly russet and the mountain itself is covered in brown bracken. Wood is being gathered in preparation for winter. It is needed already in the cottages behind the trees, where smoke from their fires is drifting across the treetops.

Richness of colour and pattern

Millais was a very clever colourist, and an excellent draughtsman. The richness in his paintings comes from his use of colour and the complicated fit of the parts of the picture. Like jigsaw puzzle pieces each part connects with the next. The detailed work in the picture's foreground brings us closely into the picture. The child and the dog look away from us across the field. Their fixed attention suggests that something is happening out of our view. What do you think it might be?

City Art Gallery, Manchester

13

The Côte des Boeufs at L'Hermitage, near Pontoise

Oil on canvas 114 × 87 cm

Camille Pissarro

LIVED:
1830-1903

NATIONALITY:
French

TYPE OF WORK:
paintings, drawings, etchings

Camille Pissarro was born on the island of St Thomas in the Caribbean. He was interested in drawing and painting from a very early age, but his father did not approve of him 'wasting his time' in this way. At the age of twelve Pissarro was sent to school in France and there he received his first encouragement to paint. When he was seventeen years old he returned to St Thomas to work with his father, but he continued to make pictures. The island gave him a new landscape to explore in paint. Pissarro met another young painter who persuaded him to travel to Venezuela and to try his hand at painting for a living. Finally, in 1855, Pissarro's father agreed to let him go back to France. He could see that his son was determined to be an artist.

A new beginning

Four years later, Pissarro met the painter Monet (see page 46) in Paris. The two artists became the central figures in the Impressionist movement. The Impressionists developed a style of painting that was laughed at for many years. Impressionism is now amongst the most popular of painting styles.

A long struggle

This painting was made about thirty years after Pissarro's meeting with Monet. It is a typical Impressionist work. It does not have a grand subject. It shows an ordinary country scene on a clear winter's day, and it does not try to make the scene prettier than it really is. Pissarro applied the paint in short, quick brush strokes, which the art world thought was very careless work, but those strokes convey a strong impression of the day in clear, clean colour.

Success in the end

Pissarro had to struggle to support his large family. He grew very weary of the battle, but he never gave up despite the hardship. His sight failed and he was blind when he died in 1903, but by then he had won public approval of his work. At a sale in 1892 more than fifty of his paintings were sold.

Pissarro was an excellent teacher, and both Cézanne and Gauguin learned a great deal from working with him.

The National Gallery, London

Songs of a Summer Night (Lynne's Garden)
Oils on carved wood and canvas 165 × 222 cm

Colin Lanceley

BORN:
1938

NATIONALITY:
New Zealander, lives in Australia

TYPE OF WORK:
paintings, with collage, prints

Colin Lanceley was born in New Zealand but his family went to live in Sydney, Australia, when he was a baby. He became an apprentice in the printing industry at the age of sixteen and an art student two years later. At college he shared a house with two friends. They worked closely together, sometimes all working on one picture. They called themselves the Annandale Imitation Realists. They tried to make pictures that reflected modern Australian life.

An influence from Papua New Guinea
The young men were interested in paintings and sculptures made by artists from Papua New Guinea. Lanceley was intrigued by the carved and painted masks and shields, which were like three-dimensional pictures. He enjoyed the way the artists had added modern materials to their traditional patterns. Lanceley found the masks particularly exciting. They had what Lanceley calls 'a presence'. He says that the way he knows that one of his pictures is finished is when he feels it has the same sort of 'presence'.

Working in collage
When the Annandale group broke up, Lanceley started to work in a technique called collage. Collage means 'sticking', and Lanceley stuck all sorts of things, even bottle-tops, to his pictures. He said, 'I felt that life could be seen as a collage, all human activity as collage.'

Leaving Australia
Lanceley left Australia in 1965. He lived in Europe, mainly in England, Spain and France, for the next eighteen years. When he returned to Australia he had worked out how he could combine painting and sculpture in pictures and he now makes three-dimensional landscape pictures.

This picture, *Songs of a Summer Night* is considered by art critics to be Lanceley's finest work. It is painted on canvas, and various objects, either found or made by Lanceley, have been stuck to the canvas. The old influence of the masks is still there. In Lanceley's use of brilliant colours against an inky black you might see a garden, rich with overhanging plants, pathways and lawns, in the still heat of a summer night. Are the 'songs' the sounds of insects buzzing in bright foliage and flowers?

17

Salisbury Cathedral from the Meadows

Oil on canvas 52.5 × 77 cm

John Constable

LIVED:
1776-1837

NATIONALITY:
British

TYPE OF WORK:
drawings, paintings, engravings

The National Portrait Gallery, London

John Constable is probably the best known painter of the English landscape. He was born in Suffolk and he loved the countryside and its buildings and people. Constable painted the countryside he knew well, spending hours out of doors, sketching in oil paint. He said, 'No two days are alike, nor even two hours; neither were there ever two leaves of a tree alike since the creation of the world . . .'

Throwing out tradition

Constable trained at the Royal Academy of Art in London. At first he worked in a traditional way, giving much thought to the finish of each picture. Such slow, careful work meant that he could not capture the fleeting movement of clouds in the sky or the radiance of sunlight. Constable wanted to paint these moments, so he began to develop his own style.

Constable's work was not well accepted until he was nearly fifty years old. His most famous picture, *The Haywain*, won a gold medal in Paris in 1824 and from that time his fame grew.

A holiday in Salisbury

Like many other painters, Constable painted some scenes again and again, each time seeing something new. He spent two happy and very busy months in Salisbury in the summer of 1820, staying in a friend's home in the Cathedral Close. He drew the great cathedral from almost every angle and later made larger, finished paintings from his sketches.

This sketch was painted in his favourite afternoon light. The clouds scudding across the sky and the broken greens of the treetops are very typical of his work. A passing cloud casts a shadow on the cathedral spire, but sunlight catches the white stonework of the tower, and shows up bright patches of red and yellow on the little figures in the landscape. We see the river through reflected greens and the brilliant patch of a white rowing boat stands out.

The sketch seems to have caught not just one moment but a stretch of time. The water flows, the clouds pass in the sky, the groups of figures pass the time of day. One of Constable's pictures was rejected by the Academy as 'a green nasty thing'. What do you think about this picture? Do you see something green and nasty or bright and beautiful?

Newcastle Emlyn
Oil on canvas 86.4 × 110.7 cm

John Piper

Photograph March-Penny

BORN:
1903

NATIONALITY:
British

TYPE OF WORK:
drawings, paintings, book illustrations, stained glass, textile design, theatre design, pottery, murals

John Piper studied law after he left school, but when he was twenty-three years of age he decided to go to art college. He became very interested in landscape painting and he also drew and painted old buildings. During World War II, Piper made many paintings showing bomb damage to buildings. One of his most famous pictures is of Coventry Cathedral after the bombing raid that destroyed it. Piper's paintings form a record of British buildings in the twentieth century.

Strength and drama

Piper's work is now enjoyed more for its own sake than as a historical record. He likes decaying ruins and elaborate buildings that have weathered over the years. Like this one, his paintings are often strongly coloured. He makes the landscape in which buildings are set bold and exciting. Skies are dark and brooding and light is often dramatic. Trees and plants are often painted in dark silhouette, standing starkly against strong plain colour. Here the red river curls under the castle on the hill like a tide of liquid fire.

Piper also loves the gentle colours of earth and stone and can use silhouettes or black outlines to produce a different effect on softer backgrounds.

Piper travelled around Britain making pictures of all kinds of buildings, each in its unique setting in the British landscape. For Piper there is no such thing as a boring place. He likes to talk to people about the places they live in, and he collects guide books, especially those written by local people. He worked with the poet John Betjeman, another lover of the British landscape, as editor of the County Guides. Piper produced photographs and paintings and wrote the text for many of the books.

'The most versatile visual man'

Piper has worked in many materials. Some of his best-known work is in stained glass. He has made windows for Liverpool's Roman Catholic Cathedral and St Margaret's Westminster and for the baptistry in the new Coventry Cathedral. He has worked in the theatre, designing stage sets, and has also designed tapestries, fabrics and pottery.

The Tate Gallery, London

The Solar Table

Oil paint on wood 60 × 46 cm

Salvador Dali

LIVED:
1904-1989

NATIONALITY:
Spanish

TYPE OF WORK:
paintings, films, furniture

Photograph Len Sirman

Salvador Dali's lifestyle as well as his paintings have made him one of the best-known personalities of the twentieth century. He was always a larger than life character, who wore astonishing clothes, made strange films and extraordinary furniture. He once made a sofa from pink satin, in the shape of the lips of a glamorous filmstar called Mae West.

An early start

Dali's life as an artist began when he was very young. His first known work is a landscape painted in oils when he was six years old. He was unhappy at the Art Academy in Madrid which he attended in 1921, and was suspended for a year for taking part in a student riot. He was also imprisoned for thirty-five days. In the end Dali was expelled from the Academy for refusing to take his final examination.

Dali's painting was influenced first by the work of the Impressionists and then by the techniques of painters such as Raphael and Ingres from the past. He also admired the way in which the Pre-Raphaelites paid such close attention to detail in their paintings. At the same time he was aware of the young painters in France who were experimenting with a style called Cubism.

Discovering the surreal

In 1928 Dali visited Paris and met a group of painters who called themselves the surrealists. They were trying through their writings and paintings to describe the way humans think 'without thinking', such as in dreams and when we let our minds wander. Dali was very interested in the surrealists' work and he began to follow their ideas. He used his cleverness with a brush and his eye for colour to give a magical quality of realism to scenes which were dreamlike or even nightmarish.

In 1930 Dali began a series of landscape paintings, placing in these scenes lonely human figures and strange objects. This painting is of a beach on the Costa Brava. It has a clear, unearthly light. Its far distant, misty horizon is made even stranger by the odd collection of objects which have invaded the scene. What do you think this picture is about?

Santa Gertrudis Bull

Oil on tempera board 83.8 × 122 cm

Arthur Boyd

BORN:
1920

NATIONALITY:
Australian

TYPE OF WORK:
paintings, ceramics, prints, drawings, stage design

Arthur Boyd was one of five children, all of whom became artists. The Boyd family was very artistic. Boyd's father was a potter, and his mother, one grandmother and both grandfathers were painters.

With so much art around him it is not surprising that Boyd started to paint early in his life. He learned mainly from his family, though after he left school he took evening classes at the Australian National Gallery Art School.

Great variety

Boyd has worked in many media. He made ceramic sculptures and ceramic paintings, paintings in oil and watercolour and, for a while, he painted on small copper plates. He made drawings in ink, pencil and pastels and prints of all kinds, etchings, lithographs and aquatints.

The subjects Boyd paints are as varied as the materials he works with. His family was deeply religious and he has illustrated many stories from the Bible. He has also found subjects in the Australian landscape and its mythology. Boyd has a real and deep understanding of the plight of the Aboriginal people and the destruction of their culture by the new world.

Boyd's techniques in painting vary too. Sometimes he works with thickly encrusted paint which he puts on in wide, wild-looking brush strokes. Sometimes he produces a surface as smooth as glass. In this picture the marks of the brush are used to show the roughness of the ground, but the paint has been put on in a calm and controlled manner.

The vast Australian landscape

This painting shows the landscape of north west Victoria. The summer sun has turned the grass to gold and the earth is baked dry. Bare gum trees stretch back towards the horizon, as far as the eye can see. An enormous space has been created, in the middle of which stands the silhouette of a bull.

The setting for the majority of Boyd's paintings is the Australian landscape. Sometimes it takes on a mysterious appearance, sometimes it is plainly described. Whatever the subject, landscapes he has come to know so well always influence Boyd's pictures.

Mont Sainte Victoire

Oil on canvas 59.6 × 72.3 cm

Paul Cézanne

LIVED:
1839-1906

NATIONALITY:
French

TYPE OF WORK:
drawings, paintings

The Phillips Collection, Washington

Paul Cézanne is probably best known for his paintings of Mont Sainte Victoire. He painted the mountain, which was near his home in Aix-en-Provence in southern France, over and over again.

Cézanne went to Paris as a young man and there became friendly with some of the Impressionist painters, amongst them Camille Pissarro. Cézanne moved out of Paris and took a house in the country near Pissarro. It was from Pissarro that Cézanne learned the Impressionist way of handling paint. Yet Cézanne developed his own style of painting, which influenced other artists who are usually known as the Post-Impressionists.

Building a mountain

Other painters have chosen to paint one place several times. Some, like Monet, were trying to capture a change of light, or the effect of different weather on the landscape. Cézanne was not concerned with these things. He was trying to find the shapes of which this landscape was composed. He wanted to build his mountain and the landscape around it.

Coloured building blocks

Many of Cézanne's paintings look similar at first glance. Several of them were painted from the same place, where a tree frames the view and a curving branch follows the line of the mountain top. When he first painted the scene Cézanne used mainly light greens and oranges, fading to pale blues and violets in the mountain and sky. This picture is one of his early attempts to build the scene. Later he chose stronger blues and deeper greens for his pictures. Here he used square, solid brush strokes for the buildings and the land, and lighter, diagonal strokes for the pine needles, bushes and grasses, and the shimmering mountain and sky. When his understanding of the mountain grew, the strokes grew bolder and the rectangles of colour became stronger. Here Cézanne has made the mountain seem far away by draining it of colour. We strain our eyes to see it. All detail is washed out. The frame of trees helps the sense of distance, too. We stand on a hill beside the trees and look out across the valley.

Matamoe (Landscape with Peacocks)

Oil on canvas 115 × 86 cm
Paul Gauguin

LIVED:
1848-1903

NATIONALITY:
French

TYPE OF WORK:
oil paintings, ceramics, sculptures, woodcut prints

National Gallery of Art, Washington The Chester Dale Collection

Paul Gauguin's early life was spent in Peru, his mother's homeland. He became interested in painting when he went to live in Paris in 1871, at the age of twenty-three. Gauguin decided to learn to paint, and after some years gave up his work as a stockbroker to be a full-time painter. By this time he was married and had five children. His wife took the family to Denmark, her home country, and Gauguin followed them and tried to make a living there. He could not settle in Denmark and returned to France, leaving his family behind.

Return to the South Seas

Gauguin wanted very much to return to the Pacific Ocean he had known as a child, and in 1891 he set sail for Tahiti. He spent the last years of his life in Tahiti, sending paintings to France and visiting Paris himself occasionally. He was often penniless and became very ill, but despite this he wrote of his life in Tahiti. '. . . After the disease of civilisation, life in this new world is a return to health.' Gauguin always tried to express himself in a way which was simple, direct and strong.

The colours of a new world

Gauguin used the natural world that he found around him in Tahiti to create brilliantly patterned canvases. He simplified the outlines of the shapes and used large blocks of flat colour. The subjects of his paintings were often the Tahitian people and their legends, but to Gauguin the landscape and the plants and animals provided more than a background to the stories. Not long after he arrived he wrote, '. . . the landscape with its violent pure colours dazzled and blinded me . . . I was seeking, seeking . . .'. He spent weeks making drawings and studies in colour to accustom himself to his new surroundings.

In this painting we can see how Gauguin felt about the landscape. He often used colour to explain his feelings about a place, and to capture its atmosphere as well as the way it looked.

Mountain Fire

Watercolour on paper 35 × 50.2 cm

John Singer Sargent

LIVED:
1856-1925

NATIONALITY:
North American

TYPE OF WORK:
paintings, especially portraits

The Tate Gallery, London

John Singer Sargent was a citizen of the United States but life had an international flavour. He was once described as, 'an American, born in Italy, educated in France, who looks like a German, speaks like an Englishman, and paints like a Spaniard.' The reference to Spanish painting comes from Sargent's admiration of the Spanish painter, Velázquez.

A new 'old master'

Sargent's mastery of paint and the elegance of his work brought him success in painting portraits of rich and famous people. For most of his life he travelled in the United States and Europe, making a very good living from his portraits, but he wanted to paint a wider range of subjects. From 1907 onwards Sargent began to paint landscapes and murals. He particularly liked painting landscapes in watercolour, like this one which shows a fire on a mountain-side.

A painted diary

Sargent painted many watercolours while on holiday with his sisters and their children. He spent five summers in the Val d'Aosta in the foothills of the Alps and during those holidays this picture was painted.

Sargent would choose a scene to paint and then complain that the task was impossible! Then he would settle down and become totally absorbed in his work, washing over the paper with broad sweeps of colour on sponges or brushes. He rarely painted skies, filling his pictures with objects or the land and trees. Here smoke masks the mountain and discolours the sky and a strange orange glow lights up the mountains. In the foreground bright flames flicker in the air as the fire eats its way down the slope.

The Brooklyn Museum, Brooklyn

No Fire for the Antelopes

Oil on canvas
N'Damvu

NATIONALITY:
Zaïre

TYPE OF WORK:
paintings

In 1943 a Belgian monk, Brother Marc Wallenda, founded a school in the country which is now known as Zaïre. The school grew rapidly and became the Academy of Fine Art in Kinshasha. There a new style of painting was born, mixing the traditions of Africa with those of Europe. One of Wallenda's students was N'Damvu.

A swirling rage of heat

In this painting fire has turned the world into a strange place where all natural colour has gone. The flames light up everything in sight. The hillside is a swirling mass of raging fire. N'Damvu has used a very narrow colour range to produce this intense heat. Dark shapes which frame it exaggerate the fieriness.

A moment of confusion

N'Damvu has caught the confusion of the moment in the movements of the hunters. Long legs, long arms, long spears are tangled so that our eyes have to untangle them. Their angular limbs are rigid with tension, and the spears in their hands make their shapes even longer and exaggerate the awkwardness. Their positions do not look natural, but they represent natural movements. One hunter appears to wipe smoke away from his face, one leans across, ready to dash.

The shapes of the hunters also keep our eyes moving across the picture. They break up the large area of fire, and make it difficult for us to look at any one part for long. Gleaming bodies frame the fire and lead our eyes to the very heart of the blaze. A fine line of gold outlines each figure, giving the impression of the fire reflecting on their brown skin. The fleeing antelopes leap through the fire in the hope of reaching safety. Rising smoke hides them from the hunters' spears.

(Visual Publications Ltd)

Plate of White Beans

Tempera paint on parchment 24.8 × 34.3 cm

Giovanna Garzoni

LIVED:
1600-1670

NATIONALITY:
Italian

TYPE OF WORK:
portraits, religious paintings, plant
and animal studies

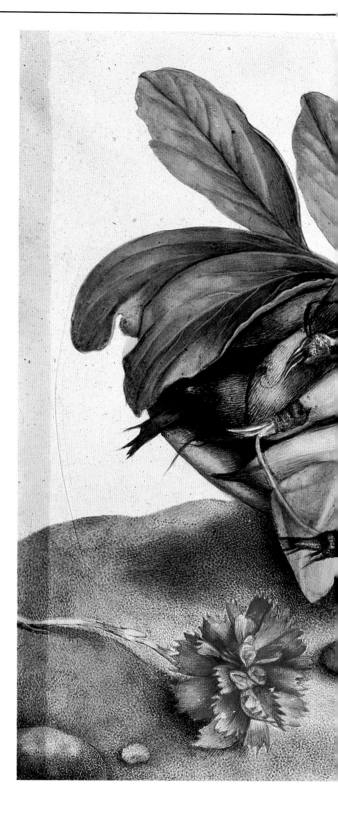

Giovanna Garzoni is best remembered for her detailed studies of plants and animals. She painted on material called *vellum* or *parchment*, which was made from the skin of a sheep or calf. The paint she used, *tempera*, was made by dissolving powdered colour in a little water and mixing it with gum or with the yolk of an egg.

Popular paintings

Garzoni was one of a number of women artists who made a living by making paintings of plants and fruits. Such paintings are called 'still lifes' and they were very popular 300 years ago. It may be that women painters chose this type of work because it requires close observation and careful technique rather than special training and knowledge about style. Very few women received an education in those days. Those that earned a living themselves had often taught themselves as well.

Finding buyers

Painters were often travellers too. They went from town to town, searching for people who would buy their work or employ them for a while. Garzoni worked in Venice, Naples, Florence and Rome. She was so successful that when she died she left a large sum of money to the Academy of St Luke in Rome, and a monument was erected to her in a church in the city.

Every detail noted

In this painting Garzoni has observed very closely and painted every detail of the simple plate of beans. The picture is very nearly life-size, so we can see the blemishes on the over-ripe fruits, the veins on the leaves, the holes made by hungry caterpillars and the shrivelled brown flowers from which the beans have grown. Three carnations add colour and they also balance the picture. Garzoni often gave her pictures an interesting ground by *stippling* (dotting) tiny paint marks on to the vellum.

Still Life: Apples and Pomegranates

Oil on canvas 44.5 × 61 cm

Gustave Courbet

LIVED:
1818-1877

NATIONALITY:
French

TYPE OF WORK:
paintings

The National Gallery, London

Gustave Courbet was a painter who insisted that painting was about seeing and he painted only what he could see. He disliked paintings of historical scenes or pictures inspired by poems and stories. Courbet was once asked to paint an angel in a picture he was working on for a church, but he refused. He said, 'I have never seen angels. Show me an angel and I will paint one'. His first famous painting was of a funeral at his home town of Ornans. Many people thought the painting was crude and ugly, but everyone was interested in it. It was the first time an everyday 'real life' scene had been painted on such a grand scale. The painting was huge, measuring 350 × 872 cm.

Politics and painting

Courbet lived through troubled times in France. He became involved in politics, and in 1871 he was sent to prison for his part in the destruction of a monument to Napoleon. While he was in prison his sister visited him and brought him flowers and fruit. These inspired him to paint and he was allowed to have painting materials. He did not usually paint still life pictures, though small still lifes often appear as details in his large paintings.

Making the best of things

In prison Courbet painted simple arrangements of the fruit and flowers which his friends brought him. This painting is more complicated than some of his other prison paintings. The fruit nestles in a chipped and misshapen earthenware dish, and a pewter jug and glass of red wine are standing beside the bowl. The ripe apples and the larger pomegranate gleam in a light which also strikes the lid of the jug. A group of apples in the front of the bowl, greener and yellower than the rest, cast heavy shadows on one side and help to give the picture a solid feeling. The fruit dish appears to be resting on a table against a dark wall, but Courbet does not give any details. He uses a rich brown colour to add to the ripeness of the fruit.

The National Gallery, London

Pomegranate Tree

Oil on canvas 150 × 160 cm

Togrul Narimanbekov

BORN:
1930

NATIONALITY:
Azerbaijani, USSR

TYPE OF WORK:
paintings

Here is another painting of pomegranates. This picture comes from Azerbaijan, a republic of the USSR which borders on to Turkey and Iran. The painting has the feel of a gorgeous eastern carpet. The pomegranate tree spreads its richness right across the canvas.

Narimanbekov was born in the city of Baku on the Caspian Sea. He graduated from a local art school and then trained at the Art Institute of Lithuania on the western side of the USSR.

A favourite subject

Narimanbekov loves to paint pomegranates and has done so many times. In this painting the ripe fruits, so ripe that one has burst open, hang thickly from tangled branches. They form the mouthwatering red centre to the picture. The skin of the split pomegranate is stretched open like a smiling mouth. It reveals not teeth but pink, jelly-covered seeds, glistening and damp.

A bold balancing act

If you half close your eyes you can see how Narimanbekov has designed the picture. He has used cool, but still rich, blues in the top and left of the picture, brilliant pinks and oranges in the centre and black and green on the ornate pot. The pot makes a very strong contrast with the rest of the picture, and yet it balances the tumbling shapes of the fruit. It is an important part of the artist's design.

A symbol for life

Traditionally the pomegranate is a symbol for life. Narimanbekov expresses joy in life in the way he uses the colour, shape and swirling movement of the fruit. What do you think Courbet would have thought of the painting? Courbet said that he would paint only what he could see. Do you think Narimanbekov would agree with Courbet? Has this artist painted only what he could see?

The Listening Room

Oil on canvas 45 × 57.4 cm

René Magritte

LIVED:
1898-1967

NATIONALITY:
Belgian

TYPE OF WORK:
paintings

© Lee Miller Archives

Like Salvador Dali, René Magritte worked in a style known as surrealism. He painted everyday objects in a plain, realistic way, but he put them in unusual places, or he changed their size, or made strange groups with them. The results are always extraordinary. The pictures are haunting or teasing, sometimes they are even frightening. Magritte mixed up indoors and outdoors, day-time and night-time, male and female. At first when you look at some of his paintings nothing seems odd about them. Then gradually you realise that they are very odd indeed.

A quiet life

Magritte's private life was very ordinary. Some of the surrealist painters lived a life which was as strange as their work, but Magritte lived quietly in Belgium. His family were quite well-off, and life was comfortable. His mother, a semi-invalid, drowned herself when Magritte was nine years old, and he was deeply affected by her death. When he grew up he studied painting at the Academy in Brussels but he did not enjoy the teaching there. He became a draughtsman in a wallpaper factory and then designed posters and publicity materials. At the same time Magritte worked on his own paintings. By 1926 he was successful enough to give up other work and concentrate upon his pictures.

A shock to make us look

This painting is more instantly strange than many of Magritte's works. It is not often that an apple fills a canvas, and here it fills a room as well! Instead of being a friendly object, which we regard with pleasure, this apple has become a menace. It is in a place which people usually occupy. Its incredible size has squeezed everything else out, and it casts a great shadow which blocks the light from the window. The apple seems to be a very living thing. In contrast the room and the scene from the window look like a picture, perhaps an illustration from a book.

Magritte called the painting *The Listening Room*. Do you think he wanted viewers to understand anything particular? Or was he just trying to shock us into thinking about the world in general, and the order that we find all around us. Or do we?

Flowers and Shells
Oil on canvas 72 × 56cm
Maria van Oosterwyck

LIVED:
1630-1693

NATIONALITY:
Dutch

TYPE OF WORK:
flower paintings

Maria van Oosterwyck was a very successful artist whose paintings sold for large sums of money. Among her patrons were the Kings of France, England and Poland. Not much is known about her private life except that she was the daughter of a minister of the church, and that she probably received a professional training at the studio of Jan Davidsz. de Heem, another famous flower painter.

A popular style
Flower paintings were very popular 300 years ago, and many artists painted them. Van Oosterwyck's work was different from other painters. She painted less formal arrangements, and her favourite flower was the large, untidy sunflower. This painting of flowers, shells and butterflies shows how very skilled she was. Can you see the dragonfly?

A careful plan
There were many special skills in these flower paintings. First the painter must be able to draw and paint the flowers themselves. A variety of flowers was included not just to make the picture interesting but to show off the artist's skill. Look at the veins in the petals of the white and yellow flowers in the centre, the fluffy seed head, the curling honeysuckle, the delicate dried grass hanging on the table edge and the shaggy striped carnation. The carnation's stripes are echoed in the ribbon-like trails of ornamental grass. However, it was not enough to paint the flowers well. The artist had to arrange them to make a graceful shape and their colours must harmonise. In this painting van Oosterwyck has chosen a range of creamy yellows and oranges amongst the soft dark colours of the leaves.

The final touches
The bouquet sits on a marbled table, which shows another skilled piece of painting. It is in a glass bottle which has been carefully chosen for its attractive reflections. Finally there are the shells, little whirls of delicate brushwork, and amongst the flowers the beautiful butterflies and a dragonfly with transparent wings.

Only twenty-four of van Oosterwyck's paintings are known to survive today, though she painted all her life.

Flowers in a Green Vase

Oil on canvas 27.3 × 21.6 cm

Odilon Redon

LIVED:
1840-1916

NATIONALITY:
French

TYPE OF WORK:
paintings, drawings, lithography

Musée D'Orsay, Paris

Odilon Redon's career as an artist was extraordinary. Until he was fifty years old he made charcoal drawings and prints, working almost entirely in black and white. Then suddenly he started to use colour. First he worked in pastel crayons and then he began to paint.

Redon had a strange childhood. He was brought up by his uncle on a lonely estate in Bordeaux in southern France. He went to Paris to study architecture but did not enjoy the work. He then tried painting, but failed his examinations. Redon then returned to Bordeaux, where he worked in an engraver's studio, learning the techniques of etching and engraving. He started to draw but his work did not sell well until he tried a form of printing called *lithography*. His first book of prints was published in 1879.

In 1884 Redon was mentioned in a best-selling novel. The hero of the novel was said to collect his drawings. Soon Redon's name was widely known.

A new outlook on life

From that time Redon's life became happier. He had married in 1880 and though his first child died, another child, a son, was born in 1889. Redon began to use colour in his drawings and then to paint in oils. His new work was as happy as his new life. He painted flowers and stories from mythology with radiance and richness. His paintings had a mysterious quality. He shared ideas with painters known as the Symbolists. They were tired of paintings which showed everything in a realistic way. They wanted to paint 'ideas', and often took their subjects from legends.

This painting of a vase of flowers has a mystery about it. The flowers are not shown clearly. It is a startling painting compared to the detail in the flowers of a painter such as van Oosterwyck. Redon's flowers could be real, but they could be the fantastic flowers of his imagination. Is it a feather or a spray of flowerlets that droops to the right, black, gold and red above the handle of the dark green jug? What is that below it? Do the buds have a strangely metallic look?

Redon's colour scheme is also very different from van Oosterwyck's. In the Dutch painting the colours, though strong, blend together. In this painting, gold, red and purple stand out in sharp contrast. Though there are no perfect petals here this picture has its own strange harmony.

Carnegie Institute Museum of Art, Pittsburgh, Pennsylvania

Chrysanthemums

Oil on canvas 81 × 100 cm

Claude Monet

LIVED:
1840-1926

NATIONALITY:
French

TYPE OF WORK:
oil paintings, drawings

Claude Monet is probably the painter most people think of first when the Impressionists are mentioned. They were a group of artists who lived in and around Paris and worked quite closely for several years, sharing their ideas and often travelling together to paint.

A new vision

Monet said that he would like to paint '. . . as a bird sings . . .', and on another occasion he said that he would like to have been born blind, then to gain his sight just as he began to paint. From the style of painting that he chose and developed throughout his long career, we can begin to see what he meant.

Careful consideration

Monet may have wanted to paint naturally but that did not mean that he did not think carefully about every aspect of his work. He always painted from real life. For more than thirty years he lived in a house in the country on the River Seine, where he made a wonderful garden. He painted the flowers and the trees and the lake in his garden over and over again.

A set of paintings

Monet often painted a set of pictures of the same subject. This painting is one of a set of four pictures of chrysanthemums, painted during 1896 and 1897. At that time Monet was very interested in the work of a Japanese printmaker, Hokusai, and he owned copies of several of Hosukai's large flower prints including one of chrysanthemums. The print may have inspired his own work. Another source of inspiration may have been a painting of chrysanthemums by the artist Caillebotte, which Monet bought after his friend's death.

Monet's chrysanthemums fill the canvas and burst like fireworks amongst dark foliage. Arranged in shaggy clusters, the texture of the paint describes their feathery brilliance as much as the colour itself. Layers of paint are flicked one on another, the tones changing sharply or subtly to build up the impression of each flower. Monet knew what paint could be made to do, and saw what needed to be done.

Some ideas

For lovers of nature

You may have read this book because you like nature. If so, perhaps you might try drawing the plants and trees or the landscape around you so that you can get to know them better. Remember Cézanne and his pictures of the mountain? Looking at the world in the way an artist does could help you to find out much more about it.

For picture lovers

You may have read this book because you like looking at pictures. If so, perhaps you would like to see the original works. A list at the front of the book tells you where to find those paintings which are on view to the public. These paintings are in collections all over the world so you will not be able to see them all. Your nearest gallery may have other works by the artists you like. Looking at the works of other artists has often given painters ideas and helped them to find a style of their own. Perhaps the same might happen to you.

For those who want to have a go themselves

You may have read this book because you like to draw or paint. If so perhaps the book has helped you to discover some of the secrets of picture making. All the work that is in the book is the result of lots of practice and very careful looking. Remember the sketches that Constable made at Salisbury? Perhaps you could start now to collect information about the countryside around you. Your notebook could help your own ideas to become pictures.